Before You Dive In

A big welcome from the Oxbridge Institute
Welcome to Oxbridge Institute, where we help you ace your exams with confidence and ease. Our mission is to empower students to excel in pivotal exams like the 11 Plus. We offer a diverse array of high-quality, interactive, and personalized online resources and materials that suit your learning style and goals. Whether you need practice tests, video lessons, mock exams, or feedback and guidance, we have it all. Curious to learn more? Check us out at: www.OxbridgeInstitute.co.uk. Don't wait, sign up today and get access to our amazing courses and programs.

What Awaits Within
Inside the pages of this book, you'll discover six engaging and insightful poems, each followed by 12 to 15 rigorous questions to test your understanding and comprehension. You'll also find the time allotted for each passage and the detailed solutions at the back of the book.

Making the Most of This Book
There are various ways you can harness the power of this book:

- Use it as 'home practice mocks' and simulate the exam conditions.

- Assign it as homework and review your student's answers with the detailed solutions provided.

- Use it to improve your reading and general comprehension skills.

Interpreting Scores and Progress

To help you interpret your scores and progress, here is a handy guide that explains what each score range means.

Score Range (%)	Meaning
91 - 100	Excellent score - the mark of a perfectionist.
81 - 90	Great score – showcasing an expert grasp of the material.
66 - 80	Good score – demonstrating a strong understanding of the content.
51 - 65	Average score – room for improvement, but not a bad start.
Less than 50	Low score - indicating a need for more practice.

Remember, scores can always be improved with dedication and effort. Let this score guide be your beacon as you navigate this book.

Poem 1: Learning to Read by Frances Ellen Watkins Harper
Time allocated: 12 minutes

This is a poem which discusses the American Civil War. The northern states (the Yankees) fought the southern states (the Rebs) over the issue of slavery. The northern states mostly believed it should be outlawed, and the southern states disagreed.

Very soon, the Yankee teachers
   Came down and set up school;
But, oh! how the Rebs did hate it,—
   It was agin' their rule.

Our masters always tried to hide
   Book learning from our eyes;
Knowledge didn't agree with slavery—
   'Twould make us all too wise.

But some of us would try to steal
   A little from the book,
And put the words together,
   And learn by hook or crook.

I remember Uncle Caldwell,
   Who took pot-liquor fat
And greased the pages of his book,
   And hid it in his hat.

And had his master ever seen
   The leaves up on his head,
He'd have thought them greasy papers,
   But nothing to be read.

And there was Mr Turner's Ben,
   Who heard the children spell,
And picked the words right up by heart,
   And learned to read them well.

Well, the Northern folks kept sending
   The Yankee teachers down;
And they stood right up and helped us,
   Though Rebs did sneer and frown.

And I longed to read my Bible,
   For precious words it said;
But when I begun to learn it,
   Folks just shook their heads,

And said there is no use trying,
   Oh! Chloe, you're too late;
But as I was rising sixty,
   I had no time to wait.

So I got a pair of glasses,
   And straight to work I went,
And never stopped till I could read
   The hymns and Testament.

Then I got a little cabin
   A place to call my own—
And I felt as independent
   As the queen upon her throne.

Q1. Why did the Yankee teachers come to the Southern states?
- ☐ a) To teach the enslaved people to read.
- ☐ b) To fight for the Confederacy (the southern states).
- ☐ c) To teach people that slavery was wrong.
- ☐ d) To persuade people to make peace.
- ☐ e) As Christian missionaries.

Q2. Why didn't the Rebels (Rebs) welcome the school teachers?
- ☐ a) They hated teachers.
- ☐ b) They were breaking the law.
- ☐ c) They were enemy soldiers in disguise.
- ☐ d) They were rude to their hosts.
- ☐ e) The teacher would take local jobs.

Q3. How did the enslaved people feel about learning to read?
- ☐ a) They didn't want to learn.
- ☐ b) They found it very difficult.
- ☐ c) They wanted to only read holy books.
- ☐ d) They were afraid to learn.
- ☐ e) They were desperate to learn.

Q4. What did Uncle Caldwell do to pages from a book?
- ☐ a) Covered them in glue.
- ☐ b) Covered them in liquor.
- ☐ c) Covered them in oil.
- ☐ d) Covered them in juice.
- ☐ e) Covered them in sugar.

Q5. Where did Uncle Caldwell hide his reading material?

- ☐ a) Under the bed.
- ☐ b) In his jacket.
- ☐ c) In the kitchen.
- ☐ d) Under his hat.
- ☐ e) In his house.

Q6. Why did Uncle Caldwell hide his reading material?

- ☐ a) He was embarrassed that he could not read.
- ☐ b) He would have been punished for trying to read.
- ☐ c) He didn't want other enslaved people to take his reading material.
- ☐ d) He didn't want to lose his place in his book.
- ☐ e) He was learning to read as a surprise.

Q7. 'And had his master ever seen the leaves upon his head….' What does the word 'leaves' mean in this context?

- ☐ a) Garden Waste
- ☐ b) Flat, green parts of a plant
- ☐ c) A dialect word for hair
- ☐ d) Pieces of paper
- ☐ e) Sandwiches with green fillings

Q8. How did Ben learn to read?

- ☐ a) He listened when the children had their reading lessons.
- ☐ b) The children taught him to spell.
- ☐ c) The teachers taught him to read.
- ☐ d) He listened when the children had their spelling lessons.
- ☐ e) He took instruction from a Yankee teacher.

Q9. 'They stood right up and helped us, though the Rebs did sneer and frown.' Which word has a similar meaning to 'sneer'?
- ☐ a) Laugh
- ☐ b) Emasculate
- ☐ c) Joke
- ☐ d) Smirk
- ☐ e) Smile

Q10. Why did the narrator want to learn to read?
- ☐ a) She had promised her daughter.
- ☐ b) She wanted to be free and independent.
- ☐ c) She needed new glasses.
- ☐ d) She wanted to be able to read letters.
- ☐ e) She wanted to be able to read her bible.

Q11. What does the expression 'rising sixty' mean?
- ☐ a) To climb up 60 stairs.
- ☐ b) Someone is almost 60 years old.
- ☐ c) Someone is ageing quickly.
- ☐ d) To drive a vehicle at 60 miles per hour.
- ☐ e) Increase the bet in a game.

Q12. What can we infer about the enslaved people mentioned in the poem?
- ☐ a) They were intelligent and driven.
- ☐ b) They were clever but lazy.
- ☐ c) They were thrill seeking and brazen.
- ☐ d) They were rebellious and dangerous.
- ☐ e) They were hard-working but poor.

Poem 2: Robert of Lincoln by William Cullen Bryant
Time allocated: 15 minutes

Merrily swinging on brier and weed,
Near to the nest of his little dame,
Over the mountain-side or mead,
Robert of Lincoln is telling his name.
Bob-o'-link, bob-o'-link,
Spink, spank, spink,
Snug and safe is this nest of ours,
Hidden among the summer flowers.
Chee, chee, chee.

Robert of Lincoln is gayly dressed,
Wearing a bright, black wedding coat;
White are his shoulders, and white his crest,
Hear him call in his merry note,
Bob-o'-link, bob-o'-link,
Spink, spank, spink,
Look what a nice new coat is mine;
Sure, there was never a bird so fine.
Chee, chee, chee.

Robert of Lincoln's Quaker wife,
Pretty and quiet, with plain brown wings,
Passing at home a patient life,
Broods in the grass while her husband sings,
Bob-o'-link, bob-o'-link,
Spink, spank, spink,
Brood, kind creature, you need not fear
Thieves and robbers while I am here.
Chee, chee, chee.

Modest and shy as a nun is she;
One weak chirp is her only note;
Braggart and prince of braggarts is he,
Pouring boasts from his little throat,
Bob-o'-link, bob-o'-link,
Spink, spank, spink,
Never was I afraid of man,
Catch me, cowardly knaves, if you can.
Chee, chee, chee.

Six white eggs on a bed of hay,
Flecked with purple, a pretty sight:
There as the mother sits all day,
Robert is singing with all his might,
Bob-o'-link, bob-o'-link,
Spink, spank, spink,
Nice good wife that never goes out,
Keeping house while I frolic about.
Chee, chee, chee.

Soon as the little ones chip the shell,
Six wide mouths are open for food;
Robert of Lincoln bestirs him well,
Gathering seeds for the hungry brood:
Bob-o'-link, bob-o'-link,
Spink, spank, spink,
This new life is likely to be
Hard for a gay young fellow like me.
Chee, chee, chee.

Robert of Lincoln, at length, is made
Sober with work and silent with care,

Off is his holiday garment laid,
Half forgotten that merry air,
Bob-o'-link, bob-o'-link,
Spink, spank, spink,
Nobody knows but my mate and I,
Where our nest and our nestlings lie.
Chee, chee, chee.

Summer wanes; the children are grown;
Fun and frolic no more, he knows;
Robert of Lincoln's a hum-drum drone;
Off he flies, and we sing as he goes,
Bob-o'-link, bob-o'-link,
Spink, spank, spink,
When you can pipe that merry old strain,
Robert of Lincoln, come back again.
Chee, chee, chee.

Q1. Robert of Lincoln is a bird. What evidence from the first stanza
supports this inference?
- ☐ a) He is singing his name.
- ☐ b) He is near his nest.
- ☐ c) He is preening his feathers.
- ☐ d) He is sitting on his eggs.
- ☐ e) He is raising chicks.

Q2. When is this poem set?
- ☐ a) In the evening
- ☐ b) In the winter
- ☐ c) In the spring
- ☐ d) In the autumn
- ☐ e) In the summer

Q3. Why does the author describe Robert of Lincoln?

☐ a) To illustrate that he is a well-dressed man.
☐ b) To argue that he is nicer than his wife.
☐ c) To allow the reader to imagine the bird.
☐ d) To show a contrast with other characters.
☐ e) To demonstrate that he is vain.

Q4. 'Hear him call in his merry note,
      Bob-o'-link, bob-o'-link,
      Spink, spank, spink,' What literary device has the author used here?

☐ a) hyperbole
☐ b) metaphor
☐ c) simile
☐ d) onomatopoeia
☐ e) personification

Q5. What is Robert of Lincoln's wife doing in stanza 3?

☐ a) Building a nest.
☐ b) Thinking carefully about something.
☐ c) Sitting on a nest.
☐ d) Watching him fly.
☐ e) Flying with him.

Q6. 'Brood, kind creature, you need not fear
      Thieves and robbers while I am here.' What does 'brood' most nearly mean?

☐ a) To want to hatch eggs.
☐ b) To sulk about something.
☐ c) To want to have babies.
☐ d) To want to create a new home.
☐ e) To build a nest.

Q7. How is Robert of Lincoln's wife different to him?
- [ ] a) She is silent, but he is noisy.
- [ ] b) He is tuneful, but she is not.
- [ ] c) She is bold, but he is shy.
- [ ] d) She is industrious, but he is lazy.
- [ ] e) He is good at flying, but she is not.

Q8. Why is Robert of Lincoln's wife plain brown when he has distinctive black and white plumage?
- [ ] a) So that she is inconspicuous.
- [ ] b) Because she is from a different species.
- [ ] c) So that she can hide from him.
- [ ] d) So that she can get food without being noticed.
- [ ] e) Because she is very dull.

Q9. How many eggs has Robert of Lincoln's wife laid?
- [ ] a) three
- [ ] b) six
- [ ] c) twelve
- [ ] d) five
- [ ] e) eight

Q10. 'Flecked with purple' Which of the following is the best synonym for 'flecked'?
- [ ] a) sparkled
- [ ] b) complex
- [ ] c) dotty
- [ ] d) speckled
- [ ] e) decorated

Q11. 'keeping house while I frolic about' Which of the following is the best antonym for 'frolic'?

- ☐ a) dance
- ☐ b) splutter
- ☐ c) create
- ☐ d) dwindle
- ☐ e) drudge

Q12. What does Robert of Lincoln's family eat?

- ☐ a) worms
- ☐ b) insects
- ☐ c) seeds
- ☐ d) grasses
- ☐ e) leaves

Q13. Why does Robert of Lincoln's carefree life change?

- ☐ a) He has to look after his newly hatched children.
- ☐ b) He has to take care of his wife.
- ☐ c) He suddenly has a lot of jobs to do.
- ☐ d) He is getting hunted by predators.
- ☐ e) He is offered a new job.

Q14. Why does Robert of Lincoln fly away at the end of the poem?

- ☐ a) He is exhausted.
- ☐ b) He is fed up.
- ☐ c) He is angry.
- ☐ d) He is migrating.
- ☐ e) He is finding a new mate.

Q15. What literary device does the author use throughout the poem?

- ☐ a) simile
- ☐ b) rhetorical questions
- ☐ c) hyperbole
- ☐ d) direct address
- ☐ e) repetition

Poem 3: O, Captain! My Captain! by Walt Whitman
Time allocated: 12 minutes

This poem is a metaphor for the death of Abraham Lincoln. Whitman was an American poet who worked for the northern states during the American Civil War. Abraham Lincoln led the northern states in the fight against slavery. Just after the war was won, Lincoln was assassinated.

O Captain! my Captain! Our fearful trip is done,
The ship has weather'd every rack, the prize we sought is won,
The port is near, the bells I hear, the people all exulting,
While follow eyes the steady keel, the vessel grim and daring;
But O heart! heart! heart!
O the bleeding drops of red,
Where on the deck my Captain lies,
Fallen cold and dead.

O Captain! my Captain! Rise up and hear the bells;
Rise up- for you, the flag is flung- for you, the bugle trills,
For you, bouquets and ribbon'd wreaths- for you the shores a-crowding,
For you they call, the swaying mass, their eager faces turning;
Here Captain! Dear father!
This arm beneath your head!
It is some dream that on the deck,
You've fallen cold and dead.

My Captain does not answer, his lips are pale and still,
My father does not feel my arm; he has no pulse nor will,
The ship is anchor'd safe and sound, its voyage closed and done,
From a fearful trip the victor ship comes in with object won;
Exult O shores and ring O bells!
But I, with mournful tread,

Walk the deck my Captain lies,
   Fallen cold and dead

Q1. Who is the 'Captain' referred to in the poem?
- ☐ a) Walt Whitman
- ☐ b) A naval captain
- ☐ c) Abraham Lincoln
- ☐ d) An army captain
- ☐ e) It is a metaphor for slavery.

Q2. What is the 'fearful trip' the author refers to?
- ☐ a) Abraham Lincoln's last voyage
- ☐ b) The American Civil War
- ☐ c) A sea battle at Trafalgar
- ☐ d) A horrible trans-Atlantic voyage
- ☐ e) A trip across America

Q3. 'The prize we sought is won.' What is Whitman referring to here?
- ☐ a) The northern states won the war.
- ☐ b) The southern states won the war.
- ☐ c) They were revered by the people.
- ☐ d) They have found the treasure they were seeking.
- ☐ e) They have won the race.

Q4. What can the narrator hear?
- ☐ a) Shouting
- ☐ b) Bells
- ☐ c) Wind
- ☐ d) Abraham Lincoln's heartbeat
- ☐ e) A storm

Q5. 'the people all exulting' What does the word 'exulting' most nearly mean in this passage?
- [ ] a) People are praying.
- [ ] b) People are distressed.
- [ ] c) People are shouting.
- [ ] d) People are celebrating.
- [ ] e) People are hopeful.

Q6. What does the narrator want the captain to do?
- [ ] a) Wake up and ring the bell.
- [ ] b) Hear the positive comments from people.
- [ ] c) Steer the ship in a different direction.
- [ ] d) Free the slaves.
- [ ] e) Be alive and well.

Q7. Which word in stanza 2 has a similar meaning to 'crowd'?
- [ ] a) Bugle
- [ ] b) Eager
- [ ] c) Trills
- [ ] d) Mass
- [ ] e) Bouquets

Q8. Where is the captain lying?
- [ ] a) In bed on the ship.
- [ ] b) In a casket.
- [ ] c) On the deck of the ship.
- [ ] d) On the ground on a battlefield.
- [ ] e) In someone's arms.

Q9. Who is the 'father' the narrator discusses in the poem?
- ☐ a) The narrator's father
- ☐ b) Abraham Lincoln's father
- ☐ c) The captain
- ☐ d) Walt Whitman's father
- ☐ e) American continent

Q10. Why does the narrator use the term 'father'?
- ☐ a) To show that they are related to the captain
- ☐ b) To show that he was their leader
- ☐ c) To show that he had created America
- ☐ d) To show his eternal gratitude
- ☐ e) To show the respect and love he feels for him

Q11. Why are many people excited and celebrating?
- ☐ a) The war has ended victoriously.
- ☐ b) They are part of a procession.
- ☐ c) The ship has docked safely.
- ☐ d) They are pleased the captain has died.
- ☐ e) They are excited to reach land.

Q12. 'But I with mournful tread....' Which of the following is a good antonym for 'mournful'?
- ☐ a) Disgusted
- ☐ b) Cheerful
- ☐ c) Depressed
- ☐ d) Fxcited
- ☐ e) Indifferent

Poem 4: John Barleycorn by Robert Burns
Time allocated: 15 minutes

There were three kings into the East,
Three kings both great and high;
And they ha'e sworn a solemn oath
John Barleycorn should die.

They took a plough and ploughed him down,
Put clods upon his head;
And they ha'e sworn a solemn oath
John Barleycorn was dead.

But the cheerful spring came kindly on,
And showers began to fall;
John Barleycorn got up again,
And sore surprised them all.

The sultry suns of summer came,
And he grew thick and strong;
His head well arm'd wi' pointed spears,
That no one should him wrong.

The sober autumn entered mild,
And he grew wan and pale;
His bending joints and drooping head
Showed he began to fail.

His colour sickened more and more,
He faded into age;
And then his enemies began
To show their deadly rage.

They took a weapon long and sharp,
And cut him by the knee,
Then tied him fast upon a cart,
Like a rogue for forgery.

They laid him down upon his back,
And cudgelled him full sore;
They hung him up before the storm,
And turn'd him o'er and o'er.

They filled up then a darksome pit
With water to the brim,
And heaved in poor John Barleycorn,
To let him sink or swim.

They laid him out upon the floor,
To work him further woe;
And still as signs of life appeared,
They tossed him to and fro.

They wasted o'er a scorching flame
The marrow of his bones;
But a miller used him worst of all—
He crushed him 'tween two stones.

And they have taken his very heart's blood,
And drunk it round and round;
And still the more and more they drank,
Their joy did more abound.

John Barleycorn was a hero bold,
Of noble enterprise;
For if you do but taste his blood,
'Twill make your courage rise.

'Twill make a man forget his woe;
'Twill heighten all his joy;
'Twill make the widow's heart to sing,
Tho' the tear were in her eye.

Then let us toast John Barleycorn,
Each man a glass in hand;
And may his great posterity
Ne'er fail in old Scotland!

Q1. Who were John Barleycorn's enemies?

- ☐ a) three monarchs
- ☐ b) the farmers
- ☐ c) the poet
- ☐ d) the people
- ☐ e) three stars

Q2. What is John Barleycorn?
- ☐ a) a person
- ☐ b) a creature
- ☐ c) an imaginary friend
- ☐ d) a plant
- ☐ e) a story

Q3. 'The sultry suns of summer came.' Which of the following is a good synonym for 'sultry'?

- ☐ a) warm
- ☐ b) lazy
- ☐ c) energetic
- ☐ d) comforting
- ☐ e) sweltering

Q4. Why was John Barleycorn left alone during the summer months?

- ☐ a) He was strong and powerful during this time.
- ☐ b) He was insignificant and not worth fighting.
- ☐ c) They had settled their differences during this period.
- ☐ d) The kings had other things they were doing at this point.
- ☐ e) They were on holiday and didn't have time to fight.

Q5. Why does the poet describe what happened to Barleycorn in such detail?

- ☐ a) To illustrate the hatred his enemies had for him.
- ☐ b) To show that the enemies were violent thugs.
- ☐ c) To demonstrate the processes barley went through.
- ☐ d) To add detail to the poetry.
- ☐ e) To argue that there was a more efficient way to do it.

Q6. Which of the following does NOT happen to John Barleycorn?

- ☐ a) He gets cut down.
- ☐ b) He gets beaten.
- ☐ c) He gets soaked.
- ☐ d) He gets stacked.
- ☐ e) He gets toasted.

Q7. 'To work him further woe.' Which of the following is the best antonym for 'woe'?

☐ a) distress
☐ b) anger
☐ c) fear
☐ d) happiness
☐ e) excitement

Q8. What product is being created in the poem?

☐ a) bread
☐ b) Juice
☐ c) whiskey
☐ d) vinegar
☐ e) flour

Q9. Which literary technique is used throughout the poem?

☐ a) alliteration
☐ b) personification
☐ c) onomatopoeia
☐ d) simile
☐ e) idiom

Q10. John Barleycorn is a well-known mythical character. What evidence is there to support this?

☐ a) The poem tells us about other stories about Barleycorn.
☐ b) There are hundreds of other retellings of this story.
☐ c) Robert Burns is a very famous poet.
☐ d) There is a lot of explanation in the poem about Barleycorn.
☐ e) There is no explanation in the poem about Barleycorn.

Q11. This poem was written a long time ago. Which piece of evidence does NOT support this inference?
- [ ] a) The poem contains old-fashioned language.
- [ ] b) There is a reference to outdated methods of punishment.
- [ ] c) People use scythes to harvest barley in the poem.
- [ ] d) There is no mechanisation for any of the processes.
- [ ] e) The poem refers to an old-fashioned figure.

Q12. Why was this poem written?
- [ ] a) To show how challenging farming was.
- [ ] b) To illustrate the importance of farming.
- [ ] c) To create a record of farming practices.
- [ ] d) To identify areas where agriculture could be improved.
- [ ] e) To argue that all farmers are violent.

Q13. Which of the following themes are NOT included in the poem?
- [ ] a) creation
- [ ] b) sacrifice
- [ ] c) death
- [ ] d) rebirth
- [ ] e) growth

Poem 5: The Inchcape Rock by Robert Southey
Time allocated: 15 minutes

No stir in the air, no stir in the sea,
The ship was still as she could be;
Her sails from heaven received no motion;
Her keel was steady in the ocean.

Without either sign or sound of their shock,
The waves flowed over the Inchcape Rock;
So little they rose, so little they fell,
They did not move the Inchcape Bell.

The Abbot of Aberbrothok
Had placed that bell on the Inchcape Rock;
On a buoy in the storm, it floated and swung,
And over the waves its warning rung.

When the rock was hid by the surge's swell,
The mariners heard the warning bell;
And then they knew the perilous rock,
And blest the Abbot of Aberbrothok.

The sun in heaven was shining gay;
All things were joyful on that day;
The sea birds screamed as they wheeled around,
And there was joyance in their sound.

The buoy of the Inchcape Bell was seen,
A dark spot on the ocean green;
Sir Ralph the Rover walked his deck,
And he fixed his eye on the darker speck.

He felt the cheering power of spring;
It made him whistle, it made him sing:
His heart was mirthful to excess,
But the Rover's mirth was wickedness.

His eye was on the Inchcape float.
Quoth he, "My men, put out the boat
And row me to the Inchcape Rock,
And I'll plague the Abbot of Aberbrothok."

The boat is lowered, the boatmen row,
And to the Inchcape Rock they go;
Sir Ralph bent over from the boat,
And he cut the bell from the Inchcape float.

Down sank the bell with a gurgling sound;
The bubbles rose and burst around.
Quoth Sir Ralph, "The next who comes to the rock
Won't bless the Abbot of Aberbrothok."

Sir Ralph the Rover sailed away;
He scoured the sea for many a day;
And now grown rich with plundered store,
He steers his course for Scotland's shore.

So thick a haze o'erspread the sky,
They cannot see the sun on high:
The wind hath blown a gale all day,
At evening, it hath died away.

On the deck, the Rover takes his stand;

So dark it is they see no land.
Quoth Sir Ralph, "It will be brighter soon,
For there is the dawn of the rising moon."

"Canst hear," said one, "the broken roar?
For methinks, we should be near the shore."
"Now, where we are, I cannot tell,
But I wish I could hear the Inchcape Bell."

They hear no sound; the swell is strong;
Though the wind hath fallen, they drift along
Till the vessel strikes with a shivering shock:
"O Christ! It is the Inchcape Rock!"

Sir Ralph the Rover tore his hair,
He curst himself in his despair:
The waves rush in on every side,
The ship is sinking beneath the tide.

But, even in his dying fear,
One dreadful sound could the Rover hear,
—A sound as if with the Inchcape Bell
The Devil below was ringing his knell.

Q1. Why does the poem begin by describing the area near the Inchcape
Rock?
- ☐ a) To set the scene for the reader.
- ☐ b) To explain the hazard in the area.
- ☐ c) To create suspense for the reader.
- ☐ d) To argue that the area was very dangerous.
- ☐ e) To demonstrate that the area was beautiful.

Q2. Why has the Abbot of Aberbrothok placed a bell on the Inchcape Rock?
- ☐ a) To let people ring his doorbell.
- ☐ b) To create a hazard for ships.
- ☐ c) To make ships aware of a hazard.
- ☐ d) To cause noise pollution in the area.
- ☐ e) To prevent ships from disturbing wildlife.

Q3. 'And then they knew the perilous Rock'. Which of the following is the best meaning of the word 'perilous'?
- ☐ a) hazardous
- ☐ b) helpful
- ☐ c) wicked
- ☐ d) noisy
- ☐ e) harmful

Q4. Why did sailors bless the Abbot?
- ☐ a) He was a kind and caring man.
- ☐ b) He often gave ships new stores for their journeys.
- ☐ c) He was a holy man, so they prayed for him.
- ☐ d) He regularly pulled sailors out of the water.
- ☐ e) He regularly saved their lives.

Q5. Why did Sir Ralph feel happy?
- ☐ a) The weather was lovely.
- ☐ b) It was springtime.
- ☐ c) He had a dastardly plan.
- ☐ d) He loved being near home.
- ☐ e) He loved being at sea.

Q6.   How does Sir Ralph feel about the Abbot of Aberbrothok?

☐ a) He respects him for his good deed.
☐ b) He admires him for his courage and skill.
☐ c) He envies him for his fame and popularity.
☐ d) He hates him for his interference and meddling.
☐ e) He fears him for his power and authority.

Q7.   What does Sir Ralph want to do?

☐ a) Give the Abbot plague.
☐ b) Anger the Abbot.
☐ c) Cause mischief in the area.
☐ d) Destroy the Abbot's plans.
☐ e) Enjoy the spring air.

Q8.   Why does Sir Ralph damage the bell?

☐ a) He hates the noise it makes.
☐ b) It is no longer needed due to modern navigation methods.
☐ c) He wants to cause trouble for other ships in the area.
☐ d) The Abbot had asked him to destroy it so he could add a new one.
☐ e) The government was going to place a lighthouse there.

Q9.   Sir Ralph is a pirate. Which piece of evidence from the text supports this inference?

☐ a) He has stolen from other ships.
☐ b) He has sailed the world.
☐ c) He has a vendetta against the Abbot.
☐ d) He has his own ship and crew.
☐ e) He has a wicked heart.

Q10. 'He scoured the sea for many a day'. Which of the following is the best synonym for 'scoured'?

☐ a) scrubbed
☐ b) devised
☐ c) discovered
☐ d) investigated
☐ e) searched

Q11. Where is the Inchcape Rock situated?

☐ a) Ireland
☐ b) Wales
☐ c) A cliff
☐ d) Scotland
☐ e) England

Q12. Why does Ralph experience bad weather as he approaches the coast?

☐ a) To create drama and suspense for the reader.
☐ b) To foreshadow the disaster he is going to face.
☐ c) To explain why they were lost.
☐ d) To argue that they should not have been sailing.
☐ e) To illustrate how changeable the weather is around Inchcape.

Q13. Why do the men wish that they could hear the Inchcape Bell?

☐ a) They enjoy hearing the noise it makes.
☐ b) They can't see where they are.
☐ c) They have been away a long time.
☐ d) They are completely lost.
☐ e) They want to apologise to the Abbot.

Q14. 'The Devil below was ringing his knell.' Which of the following words is the best antonym for 'knell'?

- ☐ a) lament
- ☐ b) paeon
- ☐ c) ringing
- ☐ d) bell
- ☐ e) hymn

Q15. This poem was written many years ago. What evidence from the text best supports this statement?

- ☐ a) The author uses old-fashioned language.
- ☐ b) The author writes about the devil, and modern authors would not.
- ☐ c) There is no modern technology in the poem.
- ☐ d) The characters are on sailing ships.
- ☐ e) The main character is a pirate.

Poem 6: The Song of the Camp by Bayard Taylor
Time allocated: 14 minutes

"Give us a song!" the soldiers cried,
The outer trenches guarding,
When the heated guns of the camps allied
Grew weary of bombarding.

The dark Redan, in silent scoff,
Lay, grim and threatening, under;
And the tawny mound of the Malakoff
No longer belched its thunder.

There was a pause. A guardsman said,
"We storm the forts tomorrow;
Sing while we may, another day
Will bring enough of sorrow."

They lay along the battery's side,
Below the smoking cannon:
Brave hearts, from Severn and from Clyde,
And from the banks of Shannon.

They sang of love and not of fame;
Forgot was Britain's glory:
Each heart recalled a different name,
But all sang "Annie Laurie."

Voice after voice caught up the song,
Until its tender passion
Rose like an anthem, rich and strong,
Their battle-eve confession.

Dear girl, her name he dared not speak,
But, as the song grew louder,
Something upon the soldier's cheek
Washed off the stains of powder.

Beyond the darkening ocean burned
The bloody sunset's embers,
While the Crimean valleys learned
How English love remembers.

And once again, a fire of hell
Rained on the Russian quarters,
With scream of shot and burst of shell,
And bellowing of the mortars!

And Irish Nora's eyes are dim
For a singer, dumb and gory;
And English Mary mourns for him
Who sang of "Annie Laurie."

Sleep, soldiers! Still in honoured rest
Your truth and valour wearing:
The bravest are the tenderest,
The loving are the daring.

Q1.   Why are the soldiers singing?

☐   a) They need to go to sleep.
☐   b) They are bored.
☐   c) They are part of a choir.
☐   d) They are rehearsing.
☐   e) They need a distraction.

Q2. 'When the heated guns of the camps allied, Grew weary of bombarding.' Which of the following is a synonym for 'bombarding'?

- ☐ a) harming
- ☐ b) sleeping
- ☐ c) flying
- ☐ d) shelling
- ☐ e) heating

Q3. Why has the author chosen words such as 'grim' and 'threatening' to describe the location of the soldiers in stanza 2?

- ☐ a) To illustrate how dangerous the landscape was.
- ☐ b) To argue that they shouldn't be there at all.
- ☐ c) To emphasise the danger the soldiers were in.
- ☐ d) To create a sense of drama and urgency.
- ☐ e) To show the reader where the soldiers were.

Q4. What are the men going to do the next day?

- ☐ a) Fight in a battle.
- ☐ b) Go home to their families.
- ☐ c) Enrol in the army.
- ☐ d) Bombard the enemy.
- ☐ e) Capture some prisoners.

Q5. 'Brave hearts, from Severn and from Clyde, And from the banks of Shannon' Why has the author described the soldiers this way?

- ☐ a) To show that they all came from one location.
- ☐ b) To illustrate that they were from all over the country.
- ☐ c) To argue that they could swim well.
- ☐ d) To show off their knowledge of rivers across the country.
- ☐ e) To demonstrate their unity.

Q6. Why did the soldiers choose 'Annie Laurie' to sing?

☐ a) They were all married to girls called Annie.
☐ b) They were all Scottish and wanted to sing a Scottish song.
☐ c) Their enemy hated it, and it would upset them.
☐ d) The sentiment of the song fits with their feelings.
☐ e) It was their favourite song.

Q7. Why might the men need to confess on the eve of battle?

☐ a) There is a chance that some of the men might die.
☐ b) They have all been guilty of wrongdoing during the war.
☐ c) They are going to commit crimes during the battle.
☐ d) They want to connect with their loved ones before they fight.
☐ e) They want to feel closer to their comrades before the battle.

Q8. What happened to the soldiers as they sang?

☐ a) It rained.
☐ b) They had a bath.
☐ c) They cried.
☐ d) They washed their faces.
☐ e) They had a meal.

Q9. Beyond the darkening ocean burned The bloody sunset's embers'
Which of the following best describes the meaning of 'embers' as used in the poem?

☐ a) The ashes of a fire.
☐ b) The glowing remnants of the sunset.
☐ c) The glowing remnants of a fire.
☐ d) The colours of the sunset.
☐ e) The smoke from a fire.

Q10. Where is the poem set?

- ☐ a) In Russia
- ☐ b) In Ireland
- ☐ c) In England
- ☐ d) In Scotland
- ☐ e) In Crimea

Q11. Why is Nora upset in stanza 10?

- ☐ a) Her partner has written her a lovely letter.
- ☐ b) Her partner has upset her.
- ☐ c) Her partner has died.
- ☐ d) She has had an argument.
- ☐ e) She has hurt herself.

Q12. 'Your truth and valour wearing' What is the best antonym for 'valour'?
- ☐ a) bravery
- ☐ b) courage
- ☐ c) terror
- ☐ d) heroism
- ☐ e) cowardice

Q13. What is the message of this poem?
- ☐ a) Sentimental soldiers always die in battle.
- ☐ b) Some soldiers are less brave than others.
- ☐ c) The battlefield is not glorious or wonderful.
- ☐ d) Being a caring man makes you a brave soldier.
- ☐ e) Soldiers who are attached to their families are less brave.

Answers

Q1.	A	To teach the enslaved people to read. The passage tells us that the teachers came and that the Rebs hated it. Then we learn that the 'masters' didn't want enslaved people to know too much and be able to read, so we can infer that the teachers were teaching the enslaved people to read against the wishes of the enslavers.
Q2.	B	They were breaking the law. The passage tells us that to teach enslaved people to read was 'agin the law', so it was illegal for them to do this.
Q3.	E	They were desperate to learn. The narrator tells us that the enslaved people picked up bits and pieces and learnt by hook or by crook. This tells us that they wanted to learn to read, even though they would likely be punished for picking up this skill. We can infer that it was very important to them and that they were desperate to learn.
Q4.	C	Covered them in oil. The narrator says he greased them, so we know he covered them in fat.
Q5.	D	In his hat. The passage tells us that Uncle Caldwell hid his reading material in his hat.
Q6.	B	He would have been punished for learning to read. We know that the enslavers did not want their slaves to be taught to read, and we also know that Uncle Caldwell went to great lengths to hide his reading material from sight, so we can infer that he would have been punished for trying to learn to read.
Q7.	D	Pieces of paper. The phrase 'leaves' here refers to the pages in a book, which are often called the leaves of a book, particularly in older writing.
Q8.	D	He listened when the children had their spelling lessons. The narrator tells us that he learnt to read by listening to the children learn to spell.
Q9.	D	Smirk. The word 'sneer' is used to describe someone smiling in a mean way. It implies that you are laughing at someone else. 'Smirk' also has the same meaning.
Q10.	E	She wanted to be able to read her bible. The narrator tells us that this is why she wanted to be able to read.

Q11.	B	Someone is almost 60 years old. 'Rising sixty' is another way of saying that someone is approaching their 60th birthday.
Q12.	A	They were intelligent and driven. We know the enslaved people mentioned in the poems were determined to learn to read. They practised whenever they could and learnt however they could. We can infer that they were intelligent because they picked up the skill of reading with little formal tuition, relying on hurried lessons and overhearing others' learning.

Test 2

Q1.	B	He is near his nest. There are several clues that Robert of Lincoln is a bird, but this is the only clue in the first stanza.
Q2.	E	In the summer. In stanza 1, we hear about the summer flowers, so we know it must be summer.
Q3.	C	To allow the reader to imagine the bird. Robert of Lincoln is actually based on a bird called a 'Bobolink', and this description enables readers to picture him in their minds and understand what the poem is about.
Q4.	D	Onomatopoeia. The author describes animal noises, which is a form of onomatopoeia.
Q5.	C	Sitting on a nest. Robert of Lincoln's wife is sitting on eggs in her nest.
Q6.	A	To want to hatch eggs. When birds want to hatch their eggs, we refer to them as 'broody'; if they are 'brooding', they sit on their eggs to hatch them.
Q7.	B	He is good at singing, and she is not. He can sing loudly, but the stanza tells us she can only sing one quiet note.
Q8.	A	So she is inconspicuous. Female birds are often dull, brown colours. This means that they are well camouflaged so that predators do not notice them, especially while raising the chicks. This is also why chicks are usually dull colours.
Q9.	B	Six. Stanza 5 tells us that she had laid 6 eggs.
Q10.	D	Speckled. 'Flecked' means an egg is covered with purple spots, similar to 'speckled'.
Q11.	E	Drudge. To 'frolic' means to move in a light, happy way, which is the

		opposite of 'drudge', which means hard. menial or dull work.
Q12.	C	Seeds. The poem tells us that he feeds his children seeds, so we can infer that this is what this bird eats.
Q13.	A	He has to look after his newly hatched children. The poet tells us that Robert's carefree life will change due to the hatching of his children.
Q14.	D	He is migrating. We know that a Bobolink is a bird, so when he flies off at the end of the summer, we know that he must be migrating. This is the option that fits best.
Q15.	E	Repetition. The author uses the line 'Bob-o'-link, bob-o'-link, Spink, spank, spink' in each stanza, and ends each stanza with the line 'Chee, chee, chee'. This is repetition to tie the poem together.

Test 3

Q1.	C	Abraham Lincoln. The introduction tells us that the poem is about Lincoln, so we can infer that he is the captain referred to in the poem.
Q2.	B	The American Civil War. The introduction tells us that this poem is metaphorical, so we can infer that the 'fearful trip' was the American Civil War.
Q3.	A	The northern states won the war. The introduction tells us that Lincoln led the northern states to war over slavery, so we can infer they were victorious.
Q4.	B	Bells. The narrator tells us that he can hear bells.
Q5.	D	People are celebrating. 'Exulting' refers to people cheering and praising someone for their actions, so 'celebrating' works here too!
Q6.	E	Be alive and well. We know from stanza 1 that the captain has died. In stanza 2, the narrator wishes that the captain was alive and well to hear all the praise being heaped upon him.
Q7.	D	Mass. The passage discusses a 'swaying mass'. In this context, we can infer that this refers to a mass of people or a crowd.

Q8.	C	On the deck of a ship. The poet tells us in stanza 2 that the captain is lying on the ship's deck.
Q9.	C	The captain. The narrator calls the captain 'father'.
Q10.	E	To show the respect and love he has for him. The narrator's use of the word 'father' is not literal. It shows that he feels that the captain is like a father to him – he feels a close bond and a lot of respect and love for him.
Q11.	A	The war has ended victoriously. We know from the introduction that Abraham Lincoln led the north to victory in the American Civil War, so we can infer that this is what the poet is referring to here.
Q12.	B	Cheerful. 'Mournful' describes someone who is feeling sad about something. The antonym or opposite of this would be 'cheerful'.

Test 4

Q1.	A	Three monarchs. Stanza 1 tells us that three kings in the East have decided that John Barleycorn should die.
Q2.	D	A plant. John Barleycorn is a personification of barley.
Q3.	E	Sweltering. 'Sultry' refers to very high temperatures, similar to 'sweltering'.
Q4.	A	He was strong and powerful during this time. Stanza 4 tells us that Barleycorn was left alone at this point as he was strong and powerful.
Q5.	C	To demonstrate the processes barley went through. These stanzas describe the methods for processing barley in detail.
Q6.	D	He gets stacked. All of the other processes are mentioned in the poem.
Q7.	D	Happiness. 'Woe' refers to sadness or distress, so 'happiness is a good antonym.
Q8.	C	Whiskey. We know that the poem is set in Scotland, a country famous for manufacturing whiskey. We also know that alcohol can cause people to behave unexpectedly, so we can infer that Barleycorn has been made into whiskey.
Q9.	B	Personification. The poem personifies the process of growing barley and making whiskey.

Q10.	E	There is no explanation in the poem about Barleycorn. The poem dives straight in with Burns not attempting to explain that Barleycorn was an allegorical figure. Therefore, we can infer that Barleycorn was a well-known figure and that Burns' readers would know of him. This is the best fit answer from the available choices.
Q11.	E	The poem refers to an old-fashioned figure. Although John Barleycorn is not a well-known figure in songs and stories, this does not prove that the poem was written long ago. All the other pieces of evidence are clues that the poem was written long ago.
Q12.	B	To illustrate the importance of farming. The poem underlines the cyclical nature of agriculture. Also, it shows the importance of farmers when it comes to producing food and drink.
Q13.	A	Creation. The farmers never claim to have created John Barleycorn. The themes of death, rebirth, growth and sacrifice run throughout the poem, as Barleycorn is killed, reborn and growing strongly until he is finally sacrificed to make whiskey.

Test 5

Q1.	B	To explain the hazard in the area. The author begins the poem by describing how innocuous the area looks, so we can infer that they allow us to see the hazard. The area is so dangerous because the rock is underwater and cannot easily be seen by the ships it wrecks.
Q2.	C	To make ships aware of a hazard. We can infer that Inchcape Rock is a dangerous position for ships, so the Abbot put the bell on the rock to make them aware of the hazard and avoid it.
Q3.	A	Hazardous. The word 'perilous' refers to a dangerous situation similar to hazardous.
Q4.	E	He regularly saved their lives. The bell warns sailors that they are near the Inchcape Rock so that they can avoid it. This means that he has saved many lives.
Q5.	C	He had a dastardly plan. In Stanza 7, we learn that Sir Ralph the Rover has a wicked plan.

Q6.	C	He envies him for his fame and popularity. This is evident from the poem, where Sir Ralph says "And I'll plague the Abbot of Aberbrothok." These lines show that Sir Ralph is jealous of the Abbot's good reputation among the seamen, and wants to spoil his work by cutting off the bell.
Q7.	B	Anger the Abbot. The author tells us that Sir Ralph wishes to 'plague the Abbott', which means he wants to anger or annoy him.
Q8.	C	He wanted to cause trouble for other ships. Sir Ralph wished to remove the warning for the other ships so that they would founder on the Rock. He wanted to cause problems for people on the ships.
Q9.	A	The poem states that 'Sir Ralph the Rover sailed away; He scoured the sea for many a day; And now grown rich with plundered store,' This is good evidence that he is a pirate.
Q10.	E	Searched. 'Scoured' means looking everywhere to find something, similar to 'searched'.
Q11.	D	Scotland. The author tells us that Sir Ralph was sailing back to Scotland and that he hit the Inchcape Rock, so we can infer that it was in Scotland.
Q12.	B	To foreshadow the disaster he is going to face. The bad weather foreshadows the sinking of the ship. It shows us that things will not go well for Sir Ralph.
Q13.	D	They are completely lost. It is dark, and they can't see where they are, so we can infer that they want to hear the bell ring to orient themselves in the area and discover their location.
Q14.	E	Hymn. A 'knell' is a lamentation or song played after someone has died. This is the opposite of a 'hymn', a joyful song played to worship.
Q15.	A	The author uses old-fashioned language. The rest of the answers tell us that the poem is set in the past. However, old-fashioned terminology such as 'quoth' and non-standard spellings such as 'blest' tells us that the poem was written long ago.

Q1.	E	They need a distraction. The poem tells us that the soldiers have been fighting, so we can infer that the singing distracts from what they have seen and done during a day at war.
Q2.	D	Shelling. 'Bombarding' means continually firing ammunition at the enemy, similar to 'shelling'.
Q3.	C	To emphasise the danger the soldiers were in. This stanza foreshadows the end of the poem, where the soldiers are involved in a battle. The language used by the poet underlines the danger that faces the soldiers every day.
Q4.	A	Fight in a battle. The author states that the soldiers have to 'storm the forts tomorrow', meaning that they are expected to leave the safety of their trenches to attack the enemy and fight in a battle.
Q5.	B	To illustrate that they were from all over the country. The Clyde is a river in Glasgow, Scotland; the Severn flows through the West Country and Bristol; and the Shannon is an Irish river. The author uses this to demonstrate that this was a regiment of soldiers from all over Britain.
Q6.	D	The sentiment of the song fits with their feelings. It was a song that every man could sing while thinking about his own loved ones. This is the best fit answer from the options.
Q7.	A	There is a chance that some of the men might die. We know that the soldiers will fight tomorrow, and traditionally, men make a confession on the eve of battle so that if they fail, they die with a clear conscience.
Q8.	C	They cried. We know that the soldiers are thinking about their families, and the poet tells us that something washed the gunpowder from their faces, so we know they are crying.
Q9.	B	The glowing remnants of the sunset. Embers are the glowing remnants of a fire. Still, the poet is speaking metaphorically here, so this is the correct answer.
Q10.	E	In Crimea. Stanza 8 tells us that the soldiers are in the Crimean valleys, so we know they are in the Crimea.
Q11.	C	Her partner has died. We know her 'eyes are dim' for a 'singer, dumb and

		gory'. From this, we can infer that her partner, who was singing and thinking of her on the eve of battle, died during the battle, which is why she is upset.
Q12.	E	Cowardice. 'Valour' refers to bravery and heroism during battle, so 'cowardice' is a good antonym.
Q13.	D	Being a caring man makes you a brave soldier. This poem was written many years ago when attitudes towards emotions were very different to our modern attitudes. Many people felt it was unmanly for men to show their emotions at this time. However, this poet argues that these sentimental soldiers are still incredibly brave and effective fighters.

Printed in Dunstable, United Kingdom